IMPROVISING
Rock Piano.

D1604483

&

Amsco Publications
New York/London/Sydney/Cologne

To my wife Beth and my son David, whose love and support throughout this project
was unfailing, even at high volume and endless repetition.
To Jim Colgrove and N.D. Smart II, my first teachers in rock time.
To Jerry Ragovoy, who showed me how to write it all down.

Cover photography by Gered Mankowitz.
Cover design by Pearce Marchbank.
Book designed by Mark Stein.
Text photographs:
Andrew Putler/Retna: page 11, Vincent Grosso: page 18, David Gahr:
pages 32, 87, Atlantic Records: page 35, Warner/Reprise: pages 38-39, 45
Sea-Saint Recording Studio: page 44, RCA Records and Tapes: page 56,
ATCO: page 67, Herb Wise: pages 71, 75.
Technical photographs by Mark Stein.

All Uncle Mike songs are ASCAP.

Order No. AM 32012
US International Standard Book Number: 0.8256.4071.7
UK International Standard Book Number: 0.7119.0192.9

Exclusive Distributors:
Music Sales Corporation
257 Park Avenue South, New York, NY 10010 USA
Music Sales Limited
8/9 Frith Street, London W1V 5TZ England
Music Sales Pty. Limited
120 Rothschild Street, Rosebery, Sydney, NSW 2018, Australia

Printed in the United States of America by
Vicks Lithograph and Printing Corporation

Contents

Foreword

To me, "rock piano" means a set of contemporary piano styles that have been associated with popular music since the early fifties. That's when the world stopped "swinging" and started "rocking." These styles are not too difficult to play or understand, and they provide lots of enjoyment for player and listener alike. They require only a modest technique, and no strenuous exercises. Basically, they are solid rhythm styles used mostly in ensemble playing, with little emphasis on soloing or extended improvisation. The modern notion of rock piano has expanded to include electric as well as acoustic keyboards, and both are included in this book where it is appropriate.

Many categories of rock piano styles come to mind: rock 'n' roll, boogie, hard rock, blues rock, jazz rock, R & B, country rock, gospel (both blues and country), to name a few. These categories are largely the invention of record companies, which need new products all the time. However, these "labels" can help you identify the feeling and musical background most appropriate to what you are playing, and I will use them as we go along. In each case, I urge you to dig deeper on your own into the roots from which the rock style emanates, and I have given you my own personal record recommendations for a start.

Rock music today is a direct descendant of rock 'n' roll, which was a combination of blues and country music. In varying degrees, rock piano styles continue to reflect these origins, and to rely on a few fundamental rhythm and harmonic concepts. Once you be-

come familiar with these concepts, the categories I mentioned will seem much more fluid, and you will soon be able to invent new rock piano grooves that suit your own special tastes.

Writing this book has given me the opportunity of sharing with you many of the musical experiences I have had over the years. As a performer and recording artist, I have played with some fine musicians for whom I have great respect. I gladly pass along whatever "tricks of the trade" I have been able to develop, in the hopes that they will smooth your way into successful rock piano playing, increase your affection for all kinds of good rock sounds, and broaden your musical outlook in general.

As a final word, I want to suggest that you take every possible opportunity to see your favorite piano-keyboard players in action. Whether Ray Charles or Elton John, Nicky Hopkins or Carole King, Aretha Franklin or Commander Cody, Leon Russell or Garth Hudson, Stevie Wonder or Barry Manilow, Fats Domino or Jerry Lee Lewis: all the great players have an intimate physical involvement with the piano which is best communicated in live performance. Besides being a treat, it'll help your playing tremendously to see how they move when they're playing well. As with all good things, if it feels right, it *is* right.

Jeffrey Gutcheon
New York City, 1978

Introduction

Rock 'n' roll grew directly out of American jazz in the late 1940s and early 1950s. By 1954, it had clearly replaced jazz as the source of our popular music, and with few exceptions, it has remained the source ever since. At the time, it represented a major shift toward *rhythm* as the core of the music. In jazz, it was common for lead instruments to play "outside the time"; in fact, getting "far out" was the goal. In rock, all playing is an expression of the rhythm.

Based mostly upon the blues, early rock was a "live" music which flourished in lounges and dance halls, particularly in the Mid-west and the South. People danced a kind of "jitterbug" to it, a dance which had been in vogue since the early 1940s when boogie-woogie swept the nation as a musical craze. (Today, the disco "hustle" is a form of jitterbug.)

The "good-time" environment from which rock sprang was important to its musical development, as the intention of rock has always been to *express* and *reinforce* the rhythmic beat. Through its techniques, rock literally generates the *power* to move people. Melodic subtleties and progressive harmonies are, for the most part, of secondary interest. In fact, "primitive" was the label most often applied by critics when rock first captivated the public's attention.

The piano was one of the seminal instruments in early rock 'n' roll, and it has emerged since the guitar-oriented sixties as the cornerstone of today's rock ensemble. But while the early rock piano giants like Fats Domino, Huey "Piano" Smith, Ray Charles, and Jerry Lee Lewis are well known, good rock piano music owes an equal debt to the behind-the-scenes keyboard men who have made memorable recordings. To name only a few, there is Allen Toussaint, the guiding spirit of New Orleans rock; Johnny Johnson, the Chicago bluesman who played many of the Chuck Berry hits; Richard Tee, our foremost gospel pianist; and Hargus "Pig" Robbins, who has synthesized the sweet-gutsy Nashville piano sound of the seventies.

For the past decade or so, as record companies have fared well with such great singer-songwriters as Carole King, Leon Russell, and Elton John, the rock world has moved from the small club to the recording studio and the concert stage. Thus, much of the "pop-rock" piano playing of today is primarily a recording and listening rather than a dancing or boogie style. Unfortunately, we'll never see these players in our local hooch clubs banging away at the upright; and on their concert tours they must take sophisticated electronic equipment along with them to recreate their records in person. But this is only to suggest that some of the "simple" pop styles you hear are not always so simple as they appear.

I love the playing of all these stylists, and I will try to give each his or her due in discussing the full spectrum of rock piano music. Contemporary rock continues to be a super-eclectic musical form that borrows continuously from its many sources and is inextricably woven into the total fabric of American music. It would be nearly impossible to describe in words the main stylistic influences upon rock players, so instead I've made a kind of genealogical chart that maps the evolution of the styles most prominent today.

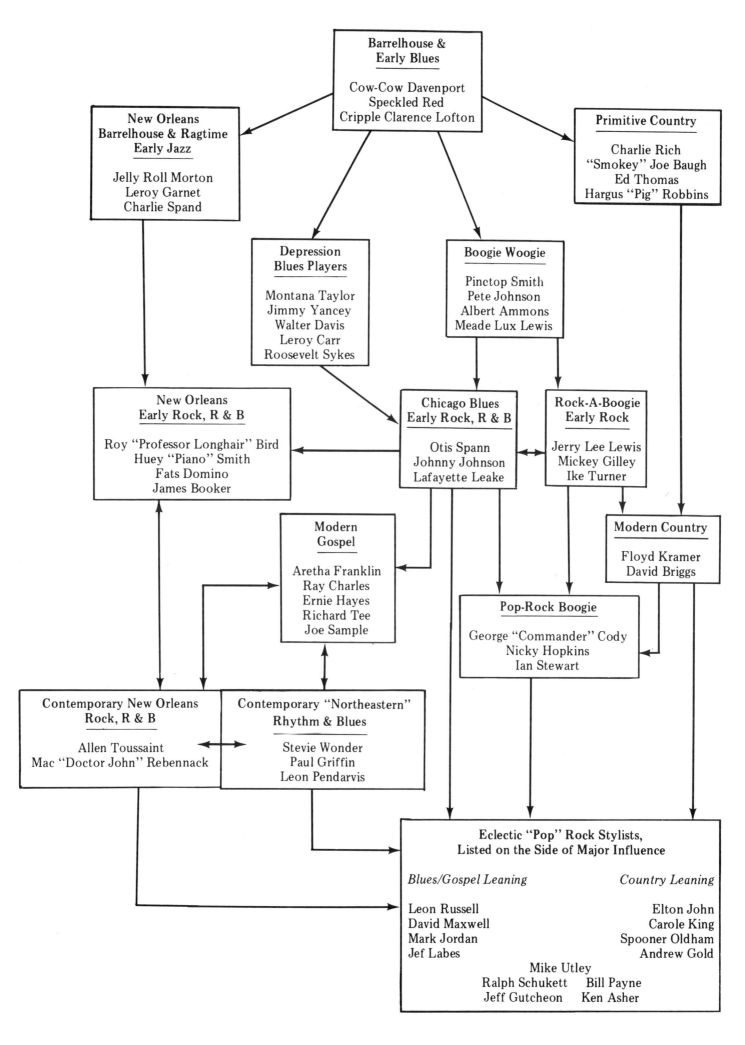

Barrelhouse & Early Blues

Cow-Cow Davenport
Speckled Red
Cripple Clarence Lofton

New Orleans Barrelhouse & Ragtime Early Jazz

Jelly Roll Morton
Leroy Garnet
Charlie Spand

Primitive Country

Charlie Rich
"Smokey" Joe Baugh
Ed Thomas
Hargus "Pig" Robbins

Depression Blues Players

Montana Taylor
Jimmy Yancey
Walter Davis
Leroy Carr
Roosevelt Sykes

Boogie Woogie

Pinetop Smith
Pete Johnson
Albert Ammons
Meade Lux Lewis

New Orleans Early Rock, R & B

Roy "Professor Longhair" Bird
Huey "Piano" Smith
Fats Domino
James Booker

Chicago Blues Early Rock, R & B

Otis Spann
Johnny Johnson
Lafayette Leake

Rock-A-Boogie Early Rock

Jerry Lee Lewis
Mickey Gilley
Ike Turner

Modern Gospel

Aretha Franklin
Ray Charles
Ernie Hayes
Richard Tee
Joe Sample

Modern Country

Floyd Kramer
David Briggs

Pop-Rock Boogie

George "Commander" Cody
Nicky Hopkins
Ian Stewart

Contemporary New Orleans Rock, R & B

Allen Toussaint
Mac "Doctor John" Rebennack

Contemporary "Northeastern" Rhythm & Blues

Stevie Wonder
Paul Griffin
Leon Pendarvis

Eclectic "Pop" Rock Stylists, Listed on the Side of Major Influence

Blues/Gospel Leaning   *Country Leaning*

Leon Russell   Elton John
David Maxwell   Carole King
Mark Jordan   Spooner Oldham
Jef Labes   Andrew Gold

Mike Utley
Ralph Schukett   Bill Payne
Jeff Gutcheon   Ken Asher

How Early Rock Became Rock

A Brief Overview

Jazz was basically music in 4/4 or 2/4 time played with a certain feeling that came to be known as "swing". Technically, this meant that you sloughed off on the tempo, playing every second eighth note in the 4/4 bar just a little bit late: it was known as "shuffling."

Borrowing from the Delta blues idiom, early rock players stretched this eighth note even further, so that a quarter note value sounded like an eighth note triplet with the second note of the triplet tied to the first:

Because rockers liked to stress the *literal* beat, rock music became polarized into 4/4 rhythms with 8 eighth notes to a bar, and rhythms with 4 "pulses" and 12 eighth notes per bar, where the beats were not sloughed but played right on time.

That polarization has continued and strengthened so that rock today is built on these two separate basic rhythmic foundations: those with a straight eighth note feeling, and those with a triple feeling. This distinction is explored continually throughout the book, and also applies to time signatures like 3/4 and 6/4 which are already in a triple mode.

Please note that I am separating the mannerisms of these two basic time feelings in early rock for instructional purposes, even though they were often closely entwined in the music itself. For example, in Chuck Berry's record of "Johnny B. Goode," Johnny Johnson (the piano player) lapses in and out of triple time on the piano because he's playing in the early 1950s Chicago blues idiom. But Berry's guitar is laying out a hard, flat eight-to-the-bar. When the Chuck Berry influence resurfaced in 1963-64 with the Beatles, all traces of the shuffle were gone, and modern rock was born.

So when you're listening to rock-a-boogie records from the fifties which sound pretty "swing-shuffly," remember: it's the *tendency* that counts.

Thigh Slapping

A Technique for Practicing Rock Body Rhythms

Thigh slapping is a great technique for practicing rock piano rhythms any time or any place. It is used by most musicians I know, especially piano players and drummers (who both play by hitting their instruments with downward motions). To get started with two-hand rock coordination, tap out the following basic rock rhythms using your open palms on your thighs. These basic rhythms and their variants will appear throughout this book with each piece, so it's a good idea to start getting them into your hands in a simple form right away. The eighth note rest sign (⅞) just marks a space that lasts an eighth beat but doesn't get played. As a rule, the left hand taps the major beats while the right hand taps the strong backbeat and special accents.

Rock Rhythm no. 1

4/4 time with a straight eighth note feeling: The basic boogie rhythm:

Rock Rhythm no. 2

4/4 time with a two-beat feeling: The basic New Orleans or country-rock rhythm, Cajun style:

Rock Rhythm no. 3

12/8 time with a triple feeling: The basic gospel and blues-rock rhythm:

Rock Rhythm no. 4

12/8 Shuffle time: The basic rock-a-boogie shuffle rhythm:

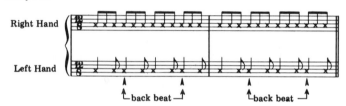

Rock Rhythm no. 5

4/4 Half time: The basic pop-rock and hard-rock rhythm:

Every song we will deal with in this book has a unique form of thigh-slapping rhythm which I will put right up front so you can think about it while playing, listening, walking about, or doing anything at all. You'll be amazed how much it helps these rhythms already in your body when you sit down to play.

Triple Feel Ballads
The Fats Domino Style

The early New Orleans style of Fats Domino is seldom invoked directly today. But it has had a tremendous effect on rock piano playing in its stark devotion to simple rhythm. I have included it here because it's the perfect introduction to the triple feel sequence in this book. It should help you understand quickly something that took me years; namely, how liberating it is to play completely *within* a groove and let the rhythm take over, almost like meditating.

In this case the bass pattern is similar for all changes, and the right hand plays eighth notes in clusters of three, 12 to a bar.

or

The challenge here is to play every eighth note with equal conviction. You should be just as comfortable playing 3 eighth notes per quarter measure as you are playing 2 per quarter. To help define this difference more clearly for yourself, play the following passage several times in a row, giving *equal time* to the quarter measure in each section. In other words, play at the *same tempo* throughout.

Now you can see why the triple feeling of "One Starry Night" is 12/8, and not 4/4 with eighth note triplets. There are never 8 eighth notes to a bar anywhere in this music, so it's pointless to write it as if there might be.

Have fun playing like Fats Domino, even if you find it a little boring. Practice playing triple feel eighth notes earnestly, because a lot of good rock playing depends on understanding this time signature. I will discuss triple feel more later.

Now take a look at the right hand in bars 10 and 13, the only places where the block chording is broken briefly by a little melody figure. In bar 13 the eighth note time remains constant; in bar 10, the octave lick announces itself briefly by doubling the time with 2 sixteenth notes, then finishes out the three-beat cluster with eighth notes. The point to remember is: *in rock, all melodic improvisation happens in terms of the rhythm—it's an extension of the groove.*

Useful Recordings

This Is Fats Domino, Imperial LP-12389 is good, but any vintage Fats Domino will do. Keep away from the later records with gooey string arrangements, as the piano is all but invisible.

Fats Domino

One Starry Night

Medium (Heavy Handed and Even Tempered)

J. Gutcheon

Early New Orleans R & B

The Straight Eighth Note Styles Of Huey "Piano" Smith, James Booker, Allen Toussaint, and Others

New Orleans, more than any of our cities, is the richest source of American musical inspiration. As even a casual visit makes clear, its music has been influenced by that of many different cultures. These elements have been so well assimilated that it would be futile to try to separate all of them, so I'll just name a few of the more prominent ones: the blues from the Mississippi Delta; dance music from the Cajuns (a subculture of dispossessed French Canadians living in the bayou country); romantic classicism from the French colonials; Caribbean island rhythms including Latin and Haitian Creole, with a strong African residue; and country music from the American South.

These influences produce certain musical effects in combination; after a while, you will begin to recognize them as distinctly New Orleans. Here are a few of them.

The "Two-Beat Feeling"

In plain language, this means dividing each bar in two. The division is accomplished by a bass move *halfway* through the bar, usually to the fifth of the chord being played. The term "two-beat" comes from country music which is generally written in 2/4 time, with the bass note alternating between tonic and dominant. In New Orleans 4/4 rock, this alternation occurs on beats one and three in the left hand.

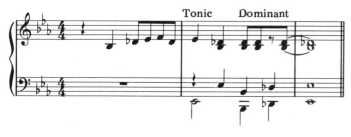

The application to dancing of the "two-beat" feeling in 4/4 time is easy to see. Your weight shifts down on ONE, back up and over on TWO, down the other side on THREE, up and over again on FOUR, and so on. The motion is assisted in the left hand by playing

the fourth beat, and in the right hand by arriving at the top of the next bar an eighth note early. This extra little kick is known as:

Pushing the Beat

Pushing the beat occurs when you play any beat an eighth note ahead of time and tie the note through the actual beat.

When used frequently, this technique creates forward momentum by stressing the offbeat as much as the beat itself, pushing ahead your sense of rhythm—rocking *and* rolling. This can be expressed in terms of accented eighth notes as:

Now try this typical Huey "Piano" Smith two-hand rhythm play à la "Rockin' Pneumonia" or "High Blood Pressure." Notice how the left hand pushes the beat for the right hand, and vice versa, rocking back and forth. Here the "two-beat" feeling is brought out even more with a typical New Orleans lilt by accenting the two-*and* and four-*and* beats, pushing one and three!

If you gave each eighth note the same accent, you'd be playing in the Cajun style.

Hot Licks, New Orleans Style

Certain piano flourishes and hot licks are associated with New Orleans rock, and I think you should develop a few of them. They are usually played at the end of a verse or chorus before the "turnaround" (slang for the pickup to the next *section*), so they can also be used as an intro. Thus, they help provide structure to an arrangement. Here is the main New Orleans lick in several variations. It is associated by now with Huey Smith, James Booker, Mac Rebennack, Ray Charles (in "What I Say"), Mike Utley, and others.

"Who's Gonna Love You?" is a piece I've concocted for you in three sections to illustrate the main motifs and mannerisms of the New Orleans style. The first section is an elementary funky rhythm style which also uses a melody figure for embellishment. Section two is completely straight, unadorned rhythm play which would be used mainly as accompaniment in ensemble play. The third section combines rhythm with hot licks to give you a taste of how to play a solo in this style.

Who's Gonna Love You?

Huey "Piano" Smith

Hooks

There are some features of "Who's Gonna Love You?" that are characteristic of rock in general, and are worth noting. For instance, the pickup is a small melody figure which then develops in bars 2, 4, 6, and 12 as the changes of the verse are introduced.

And as you have seen, the turnaround between sections contains the main New Orleans hot lick and its variants. When used *consistently* in this way, melody and rhythm figures are known as hooks.

Hooks give your playing and arranging a *structure* which provides clarity for the listener by marking your progress through a tune. If you always play the same (or similar) phrase at the pickup or turnaround, people will know a verse is coming (or ending) and will appreciate you for providing this additional key to understanding your music. I think this use of the word hook is record-industry jargon meaning "something to hang your hat on." I have used many kinds of hooks throughout the book. Some are notated in the music, and some aren't. But keep your ears open for them and try to develop an instinct about using them.

Useful Recordings

Check your Oldies but Goodies shop for records by: *Huey "Piano" Smith, Chris Kenner, Barbara George, Jesse Hill, Earl King,* and *Ernie K-Doe.* All were recorded in New Orleans in the mid-to-late Fifties, and the stylistic consistency is excellent.

Eight-To-The-Bar Rock Boogie

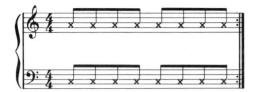

Eight-to-the-bar boogie-woogie originated in Kansas City in the late 1930s and became a worldwide smash in the ensuing years. Its foremost exponents were Pete "Roll 'em Pete" Johnson, Albert Ammons, Clarence Lofton, and Pine Top Smith, who is generally credited with coining the phrase boogie-woogie. If I had to choose the two or three most important precursors of rock, this would surely be one of them. Here is the beginning of that hard-driving eighth note time and get down playing style that we associate with rock music today.

To play this style successfully you have to keep thinking *down*; keep pushing those eighth notes *down* hard, with equal intensity and attack. The musical brilliance in rock-a-boogie comes from its note combinations. Rhythmically, it's "straight ahead" all the way, and really simple to play once you get going.

The key to playing eight-to-the-bar boogie is a strong, independent left hand. The *same* bass figure—this one, for example,

is repeated in each of the standard blues changes. These are: the tonic (root), subdominant (fourth), and dominant (fifth) chords of any major key (often referred to as the I, IV, and V chords). Before going any further, read through "Sweet Little Fourteen" playing only the left hand. Take a moderate tempo at first until your hand gets used to this kind of repetitive groove, and try to play with an aggressive evenness.

Notice that the bass pattern shifts on the second and fourth beats of each measure. These are known as the "back beats"—That's where the percussionist usually plays a snare shot in rock. Back beats are always emphasized by motion in boogie-woogie basses such as these:

or

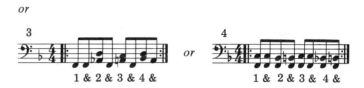

Now that you have steady eighth note left-hand figures clearly in mind, the rhythm patterns of right-hand play can be easily understood. There are three basic options.

Option no 1: Play all the eighth notes with equal emphasis (like the left hand):

Option no. 2: Emphasize the main beat:

Option no 3: Emphasize the "off" and beat:

To improvise boogie-woogie successfully, just combine these three rhythm options. Here are some simple rules for how to do it:

Rule A
To change emphasis from main beat to off beat, strongly accent the first off beat you wish to play and *tie it over* through the next main beat (eighth note), accenting all successive off beats.

Rule B
To change emphasis from off beat back to main beat, accent both in succession, and just the main beats thereafter.

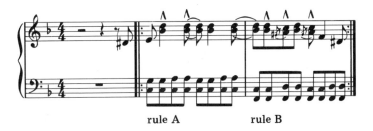

rule A   rule B

If you find the finger constructions as noted above self-explanatory, try "Sweet Little Fourteen," a fourteen-bar boogie I wrote reminiscent of the style played on the old Chuck Berry records by Johnny Johnson, Lafayette Leake, and Otis Spann. Otherwise, turn to the chapter on Blues Rock Fingerings for a more complete discussion.

Useful Recordings

The *Chuck Berry* masters have been packaged and re-packaged many times by Chess records. *Chess LP-1465* has a nice assortment. The piano players on the best known hits were:

Johnny Johnson:
Maybelline, Roll Over Beethoven, School Days.

Lafayette Leake:
Rock 'n' Roll Music, Oh Baby Doll, Sweet Little Sixteen, Johnny B. Goode.

Otis Spann:
You Can't Catch Me, No Money Down.

Sweet Little Fourteen

Introduction

J. Gutcheon

8 Rock-A-Boogie Shuffle

The Memphis Style of Jerry Lee Lewis

Jerry Lee Lewis is a masterful rock-a-boogie player famous for his machine-gun-like eighth note attack, and his percussive right-hand swoops up and down the piano (glissandi). He was among the true pioneers of the "triple feel" boogie-woogie style in early rock with recordings like "Whole Lot Of Shaking Going On."

Although the harmonies and fingerings of 12/8 boogie-woogie are much like those of the eight-to-the-bar style, you may find it harder to play, especially in the solo sections. This is just because there are *more* notes per bar than in 4/4 time, which requires better shoulder, wrist, and forearm development (see appendix).

Left-Hand Play

The left hand in 12/8 Boogie is written as a shuffle, with the first and second eighth notes tied so that they become a quarter note. Ordinarily, the shuffle feeling would require that you accent the first eighth note, and play the last one more lightly, giving a "lift" to the rhythm.

Accents for ordinary shuffle

To rock this correctly, however, accent *all* the bass notes equally and strongly. It's tougher on the hand, but it's right for the rhythm.

Accents for rock shuffle

Playing the Glissandi

Have you ever wondered how to play those hand runs *à la* Jerry Lee that go ZZZZING! back and forth over the treble? They sound easy but they're tough to do because your fingers are so much softer than the keys. To minimize the pain and damage, take as much of the pressure as possible on your *fingernail*. The correct hand positions, both ascending and descending, are shown in Figures one and two. For greatest efficiency, the center of your fingernail should strike the

key where its top and side meet (which side will depend on which direction you're going).

Fig. 1

Fig. 2

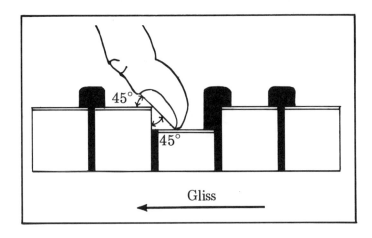

Gliss

Uses of the Glissando

The Jerry Lee style glissando has several uses in good rock playing. The first and most obvious is for dramatic effect: it's *flashy*. In addition, it *cuts through*, and being heard while electric guitars are playing can be a problem for keyboards. Use the gliss with confidence, and LEAN on it.

The glissando can also be a great way to *change registers* instantly without having to play an elaborate finger passage, (bars 10, 11) or to *change mood* (bars 17, 18) like an attention-getting spacer.

This piece has been written in two distinct parts. The first twelve-bar chorus is a small compendium of rhythm accompaniment figures used in ensemble back-up playing. Taken out of context so you can investigate them individually, they make up a kind of list.

1. Bars 1-4

2. Bars 5, 6

3. Bars 7, 8

4. Bars 9, 10

5. Bars 11, 12

To master this style, practice playing a whole twelve-bar chorus using only one of the figures, transposing the chord inversion with the changes. Repeat for each of the other figures. You can see what great flexibility you have playing rhythm alone. A few empty staves are provided for you to invent your own rhythm figures or write down others you hear.

The second section is a real Jerry Lee Lewis solo. Wait until you've been playing rhythm a while before trying it. Obey the tempo marking and only play this as fast as you now can. Work it up to tempo in time.

Useful Recordings

Jerry Lee Lewis - Original Golden Hits (4 volumes) on Sun Bellaphon has it all.

Jerry Lee's Boogie

pretty damn fast
(as fast as you can play)

J. Gutcheon

Blues Harmony/Time vs. Country Harmony/Time

The difference between blues and country music is an attitude which seems to apply equally well whether you are talking about rhythm or harmony. As I see it, blues time differs from country time in the *same way* that blues harmony differs from country harmony. Let me try to illustrate this difference.

Country music is played with a classical sense of time; that is, right *on* the beat. Blues music, on the other hand, tends to be played on the *back end* of the beat. Country time is known as "square time"; blues time is called "laid back," or "leaning back." To complete the picture, some rock music (and *all* disco music) is played toward the *front end* of the beat and is "leaning forward."

If you are unfamiliar with thinking about a beat as having a middle, or a front and back end, try visualizing it this way. Let's say you are playing at a tempo equal to a metronome setting of eighty beats per minute. Thus in literal time value, each beat has three-quarters of a second alloted to it.

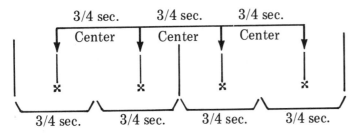

The time it takes you to strike a note, (a fraction of a second) is—obviously—much smaller than the three-quarters of a second taken up by the whole beat. As you can tell from the diagram, you have considerable latitude as to where in the beat the note gets played: front, dead center, or back end.

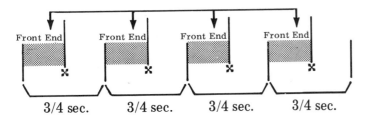

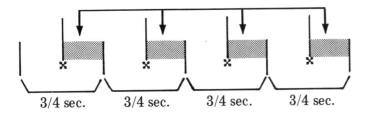

The secret to playing good time is consistency. Whichever attitude you take, blues or country, stick to it. Play a whole tune laid back and it will sound funky; slightly ahead of the beat and it will sound aggressive. If you vary between one and the other, it will merely sound erratic and indecisive, as if your sense of time were poorly developed.

As blues time is laid back or played slightly *behind* the beat center, blues tuning, especially in guitars, tends towards the *underside* of the note and blues harmonies rely on *lowering* the important intervals of the tonic chord a half tone*. The dominant seventh, in fact, is usually played and always implied in the tonic chord.

In piano blues runs or licks, these lowered tones (sometimes called "blue notes") are used as passing tones away from or back to the interval to which they refer:

Since pianos can't bend notes like guitars or the human voice, they instead quickly alternate back and forth or strike adjacent notes at the same time:

I've introduced the idea of blues harmonies this way for a special reason: I don't want you to think that these blue notes—the flatted (or minor) third, the flatted fifth, and the flatted (or dominant) seventh—are all there is to blues harmony and that any time you play one it's O.K. What's important is the *juxtaposition* of the blue note with its interval, the constant movement between one and the other, and the tonal

* To develop your ear so that it's sensitive to this, listen alternatively to a blues and a country record in the same key (D major would be good).

28

ambiguity created. Blues music is the simultaneous major-minor feeling that results from this kind of playing, and you'll find constructions like this in the blues derivative rock throughout this book.

By comparison, country tunings tend, if anything, to be right on the note or even slightly sharp. Country harmonies (not the Applachian Mountain variety which are modal and *do* resemble blues) are straight from the hymnbook, and a clear distinction is drawn between major and minor. Accidentals used to create blue notes are almost totally absent in country music, and the dominant seventh or dominant ninth, so important in the blues is used more traditionally: to resolve a chord up a fourth or down a fifth.

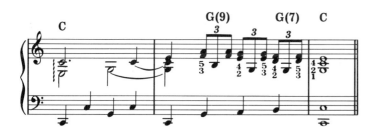

Country harmonies for the piano clearly derive from the fact that until recently, country music was made almost exclusively by stringed instruments. Indeed, the country piano style evolving today borrows liberally from guitar, banjo, and mandolin tunings and idioms. In the following examples, notice that important chords (I, IV, and V) are often played as simpler fourths or fifths, rather than as the more familiar three-note triads.

You may have noticed the use of whole steps as transitions between the open fourths and fifths. This is the piano equivalent, generally attributed to Floyd Kramer, of the hammer-on, pull-off technique common to guitar playing. In hammering on, an open string is plucked, then fretted up a whole tone, thereby raising the pitch. In pulling off, a fretted note is let go, and the pitch reverts to that of the open string.

Because of the piano's flexibility, this technique can be used in many ways to sound really beautiful.* Here's a little exercise showing how you can hammer-on and pull-off to seconds, thirds, and sixths, as well as to fourths and fifths (the intervals are noted).

To conclude this section by relating it all back to rock, here are two passages virtually identical in rhythmic construction that you can have some fun with. One is written in a blues style, the other in a country style. Once you catch on to the notes, try playing the country passage laid back. If you succeed you'll be playing country blues. Then try playing the blues passage leaning forward—and you'll be playing blues rock!

blues passage

country passage

* A word or caution: this technique is so easy to learn and seductive that you may want to use it everywhere. Don't forget that it's only a part of the country rock bag, and pay close attention to your two-hand rhythm playing.

Blues Rock Fingerings

Blues constructions for the right hand involve unorthodox fingerings which are not always easy to figure out by yourself. If you have had classical training, blues licks may feel very uncomfortable to your hand. However, once you understand the techniques—and the reasons for them— a little practice will eliminate further difficulty.

To improvise blues licks successfully, you must have mobility *up* and *down* the keyboard. There's nothing as frustrating as hearing a great lick in your head and not knowing how to get there or stumbling on the way. This chapter develops a working vocabulary of blues fingering methods which can be used in extensive combinations.

Blues licks tend to be simple, direct melodic progressions from one of the major blue intervals to another. These intervals are: the major or minor third, the flatted or perfect fifth, and the dominant seventh or dominant ninth. These licks fall into several main categories (the intervals are noted):

Runs of Parallel Thirds

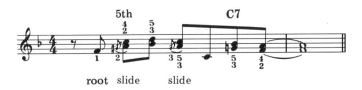

Runs Combining Parallel Thirds and Sixths

Runs Using Arpeggios

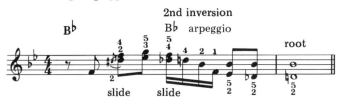

Runs of Octaves

Fifth finger & thumb throughout

The Half-Tone Slide

Rule A: Going up from a black key to a white key.

Examples 1 and 3 above contain a common blues figure called the half-tone slide, in which you quickly raise a note by a half-tone. Often you can't use two adjacent fingers to do this without immobilizing your hand for further use. This happens when you go from a black key up to the next white key. In such cases (mostly thirds) you have to play both notes with the *same finger*. Here are several instances where the slide occurs. Practice it using the second, third, or fourth fingers as noted. As the chapter progresses, you'll discover when each finger is required.

The same slide fingerings may apply where other intervals are involved, sixths and fourths in this example:

Rule B: Going up from a white key to a black key or from a white key to a white key.

In keys where similar note sequences require going up from a white key to a black key, or a white to a white, two fingers must be used for the half-tone slide—the index and third, or the thumb and index fingers.

In many cases you need to use both same-finger and two-finger half-tone slides in close proximity to play a lick. It's easy if you just follow the rules.

Let's go a step further with an improvisational case study. Suppose you are in a playing situation like the one below, where several different fingers may be used for the same slide: which one do you choose? The answer depends on whether you want to take your improvisation up or down the keyboard. If you want to go *up*, you'll need fingers available on the *right* side of your hand, so slide with your index finger, and keep "walking" up the keys.

Similarly, if you want to go *down*, slide with the third or fourth finger, leaving fingers available for play on the *left* side of your hand. This example illustrates both directions in the same passage.

Boogie in C

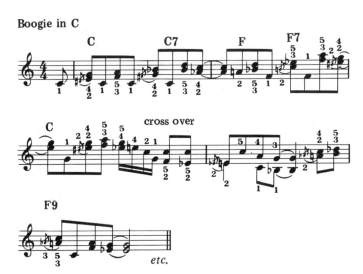

Cross-over Licks

The example you have just played, as notated, employs a technique especially useful in descending runs that I call cross-over licks. In principle, they're just like descending scales where you have to cross over your thumb, and they enable you to play some flashy licks effortlessly. Here are several; some of them are used in the book and others are substitutes you can use in similar situations. This method is quite simple, and you'll soon be able to invent your own.

Moderate boogie

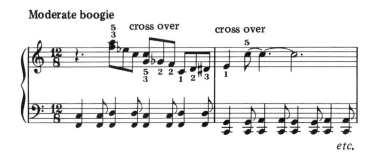

Slow & lowdown

Quick boogie

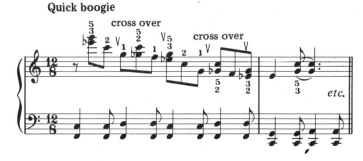

Finally, there's a kind of two-finger blues lick you should know about. I regard it as the "cheap thrill" of blues playing and don't include it in any of the example pieces, but it's o k for making quick time up and down the keyboard in some contexts. I leave it to you to apply.

31

Ray Charles

6/4 Blues-Gospel Style

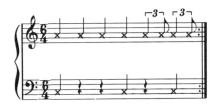

The 6/4 blues-gospel style is the kind of piano music you often hear on R&B songs like "Do Right Woman," Aretha Franklin's hit by Chips Moman; and also on "Peanuts and Diamonds," Bill Anderson's country hit. Sometimes known as a "gospel waltz," the 6/4 bar is just twice the length of a normal 3/4 bar with the back-beat usually played on the fourth beat, the beginning of the second pulse.

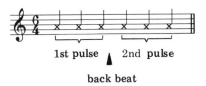

As the 6/4 blues-gospel style emanates from a church context, it has certain deliberate dramatic or "theatrical" characteristics designed to carry well in large spaces and *lead* a congregation. Some of these are explored below. Stark contrasts in mood—alternately tempestuous or soothing—are common in this kind of playing, although they depend on your own feeling and are not easily notated.

Gospel tempos are usually slow and reverential, but in a shouting spirit they may get as fast as a bright shuffle. Stylistically, the playing is the same. However, at slower tempos there is usually no syncopation. Well-known piano players considered adept at this style include Aretha Franklin, Ray Charles, Richard Tee, Joe Sample, Ernie Hayes, and of course the real every-Sunday church players who don't make popular records. I have always considered the famous Motown shuffle (heard in tunes like "How Sweet It Is") to be essentially a gospel style.

The main rhythmic feature of the 6/4 blues-gospel style is the use of triplets to subdivide each beat. An ordinary 6/4 bar looks like this:

However, the basic rhythm structure in 6/4 gospel is:

As we have seen before, the shuffle arises in triplet configurations when the second note is tied to the first:

This shuffle underpinning is usually right there from the pickup, setting the pace.

Thereafter, the shuffle contributes to the "theatrical" effect by weaving in and out of the overall straight sense of 6/4 time. In other words, as you see in bars 3 and 4, it can be used for *effect:*

Keeping the triple feel shuffle in mind, try this brief "blues hymn," plodding at first until you get used to some of its mannerisms.

Only His Love

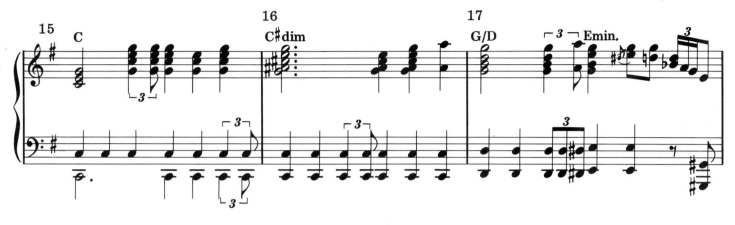

Aretha Franklin

Octave Runs

I'm sure you noticed the flashy octave runs in both bass and treble. These are generally used to announce an important chord change, such as the G to E minor, and E minor to B minor in bars 8, 9, and 10.

"Backward" Resolutions

One harmonic trick in gospel playing that you can use with confidence is what I call the "backward resolution." This means changing a chord down a fourth in the root position. For example, change to a G chord with a C chord; change to an A chord with a D chord; and back to a D with a G chord.

Likewise, in the gospel style, if you have to lay on a chord for a few extra beats, shift quickly up a fourth and then resolve back again; it's effective and evocative (see bars 1, 4).

The total effect of these octave runs, blues licks, and full chords lifted by the shuffle feeling, is a declarative style which is great for accompanying group sings, and is fairly easy to play.

Useful Recordings

Record examples here are scattered. In general; *Aretha Franklin's Greatest Hits*, Atlantic SD 8295; also, *Ray Charles*, *The Genius Sings the Blues*, Atlantic 8052; *The Crusaders*, Blue Thumb BTS 6007, especially "Hard Times." Keep your ears open.

The "Straight-Eight" (Eighth Note) Gospel Style

The eighth note gospel style is a super energetic, highly percussive, forward-leaning style which, although not difficult to understand, is not necessarily easy to play. The rhythmic essence of the style, simply put, is that the eighth note (not the quarter note) is the basic unit of time. The tempos range from bright to speedy.

Eighth note gospel playing is beginning to emerge as a distinct popular style now in the capable hands of Richard Tee on such records as Paul Simon's "Gone At Last," Joe Cocker's "I Broke Down" (our example piece by Matthew Moore), and "Stuff." But it's been around for years and is an important ingredient in the playing of pop favorites like Elton John, Leon Russell, and Nicky Hopkins, as well as a continuing R&B mainstay.

The most severe limitations in playing this style are physical. It requires muscular, well-developed shoulders, forearms, wrists and hands—and a piano with a responsive action. If your instrument is from the Depression days or before, with lots of dust in the wippens, be careful: a quick blast could cause it serious internal injuries, and cost you lots of money.

The key feature in straight-eight gospel is *hand* play, as distinct from *finger* play. The right hand usually moves as a *unit*, which requires limited finger dexterity:

You'll notice that the second of these right-hand runs begins on the offbeat (the eighth note after the beat), effectively "setting up" the *next* beat since we're always listening for the one-two-three-four. This aggressive device is heightened by alternating a weak sixth chord on the offbeat with a strong dominant ninth on the beat.

Now let's add the left hand, because two-hand interplay is really what generates the urgent forward motion in gospel music. The main point to remember is that the left hand *keeps steady time* while the right hand is syncopating. In this example, the fifth finger and thumb rock octaves, the thumb steadily accenting the offbeat.

Here is the same passage in a busier, "pushier" version. With the syncopated sense shortened to sixteenth notes, the main figure gets an added half turn per bar. It doesn't sound crowded, however, because the rhythm feels "cut," or twice as fast.

This series of staccato sixteenth-note beats can be intensified with a kind of two-handed "chase." In this case, the hands play a parallel construction with the left hand playing eighth note octaves and the right hand anticipating each octave by a sixteenth note—as if it were chasing the left.

Play the "chase" over and over.

A helpful hint: as you play this piece, tap your heels in eighth note time, and do an eighth note shimmy on the piano bench. You'll find it easier to intuit this anticipative style if your whole body is rocking from side to side with the basic rhythm.

Useful Recordings
Look for Richard Tee credits, especially on R&B records produced by Jerry Wexler and Jerry Ragovoy. Also, *Joe Cocker, Stingray*, A&M SP 4574; *Paul Simon, Still Crazy After All These Years*, Columbia PC 33540, and Tee's own group, *Stuff*, Warner Bros. BS 2968.

Stuff - Gordon Edwards, Eric Gale, Cornell Dupree, Richard Tee, Chris Parker and Steve Gadd.

I Broke Down

The Straight-Eighth Note Rhythm And Blues Style

The term R&B has been loosely used to describe that whole genre of popular music which is "funky" (syncopated) and owes its harmonic derivation to the blues. From that point of view, of course, the various New Orleans, early rock, and gospel styles can all be considered R&B—and indeed they are. In contemporary jargon, however, R&B is more narrowly defined by some particular rhythmic and harmonic tendencies.

Rhythmically, modern R&B makes interesting use of the sixteenth note in a basic 4/4 context. In ensemble playing this is often expressed as either sixteenth notes on the high-hat cymbal, or "chicken-pickin'" in the rhythm guitar; and it can become a very "nervous" soul style suitable only for electric keyboards or synthesizers. (See "One-note linear grooves.")

More often, though, the rhythm core is the familiar straight eighth notes over a quarter note base, with the sixteenth note feeling used as a high energy "passing gear" for hot licks and special rhythm figures. This gives rises to a wonderful *layered time effect* in the music which the piano can exploit with its great flexibility.

base

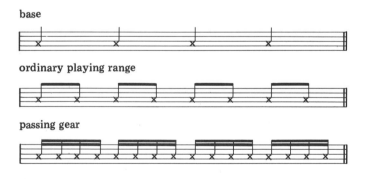

ordinary playing range

passing gear

Now take a quick pass at excerpts from our example piece, "What Is Success?" by Allen Toussaint, to see how easily you can shift up and down from eighth note playing and how each is deployed in this rhythmic style.

Now that you have some of the blues-playing slides, slurs, and techniques in your fingers and ears, you can confront the pentatonic scale, which I deliberately steered you away from earlier.

The chord construction of R&B tunes is largely based on pentatonic intervals, so this gives us an excellent chance to broaden our discussion of blues harmonies.

The pentatonic scale is the group of intervals between five notes represented by the black keys on the piano.

As a mode, these intervals form the basis for the native music of peoples as diverse as the Scottish and the East Indian, the African and the Chinese, the Japanese and the American Indian. So clearly, the pentatonic scale comprises universally congenial sounds.

This scale was simplistically labelled "the blues scale" back in the 1950s be-bop days because it offered a short cut to blues playing that fit in with the harmonic taste of that era for raised ninth and thirteenth chords. For example, consider this passage in which the pentatonic scale beginning on E flat is applied indiscriminately ad nauseum to standard blues changes:

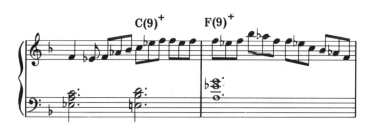

I find this a kind of formula playing too predictable and stilted for my own tastes.

But look what majestic tonal vistas open up if you simply use the same notes of the pentatonic scale as the roots of a series of major chords:

Now let's take this progression one step further in the direction of the blues by playing each chord as a dominant seventh, ascending by nearest inversions. You'll quickly recognize these chord changes when you play "What Is Success?"

Since R&B composition rests firmly on these pentatonic scale intervals, I guess that qualifies it as "primitive" music, no matter how sophisticated it gets. For more evidence of this R&B—pentatonic influence on pop composition, both primitive *and* sophisticated, here are the release from "Jumping Jack Flash" (Rolling Stones) and the main theme from Lennon & McCartney's "I am the Walrus." (Both examples are preceded by the pentatonic scale to which the changes belong.)

Allen Toussaint

In addition to Mr. Toussaint, who remains a prime mover in New Orleans R&B, other prominent R&B keyboard stylists you should know include Joe Sample of the Crusaders in L.A., Richard Tee, Ernie Hayes, Paul Griffin and Leon Pendarvis in New York.

Useful Recordings

Bonnie Raitt, Streetlights, Warner Bros. BS2818; *Howard Tate*, Atlantic SD 8303: In general, the Atlantic "Black Gold" series, and Aretha Franklin records from 1968-1972.

What Is Success?

Arpeggiated Ballad Style

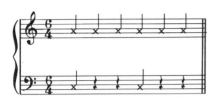

There is a beautiful ballad style for the piano in 6/4 tempo which will deepen your understanding of this time signature and give us an excellent opportunity to discuss some concepts of arranging for rock piano. The arpeggiated style, which you hear Booker T. Jones playing on Otis Redding's recordings of "You Don't Miss Your Water" and "I've been Loving You Too Long," has both classical and gospel roots. Because it is a simple, spare style that uses relatively few notes or flourishes, it can be invested with a great deal of feeling: thus its suitability for ballads, and for bringing out the piano's rich overtones, which are often lost in faster rock tunes that require a more percussive effect.

An arpeggio is simply a chord spelled out note by note, with each note given a specific duration:

The application of arpeggios in a 6/4 rock 'n' roll context is easy to see. Since each measure has two pulses, the arpeggio's simplest form is three notes up and three notes down. These six notes can outline a triad (including it's octave) in any inversion:

Arpeggiated inversions of G Major Chord

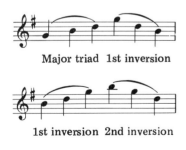

Major triad   1st inversion

1st inversion   2nd inversion

2nd inversion   Major triad

This fact alone gives rise to a remarkable arranging technique: you can create drama in your piano part merely by controlling how you change inversions! In this piece by Steve Goodman, for example, the whole first verse spells out the chords in the most direct possible fashion, starting in the root position. To keep the mood quiet, each chord change is made in the inversion closest to the notes of the preceding chord, so that you never move more than the interval of a second in either direction. In the second verse, more excitement is generated by moving the whole sequence up to higher inversions, and continuing in that direction. I've written out the chords in all three verses so you can see what I mean:

First verse

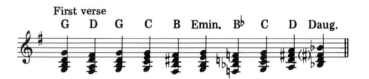

Second verse

last verse

Additional excitement is added by playing the arpeggiated tones together with other notes in the chord, creating a resonant ringing effect which can be enhanced by a measure-long use of the sustaining pedal.

The intensity of the arrangement is increased from the middle of the second verse through the bridge by using left-hand runs to make important changes. Since there is little left-hand movement in the piece otherwise, this minimal activity lends considerable emphasis.

left hand run

Gospel lick   Left hand run

With the addition of a few gospel licks like the one in the previous example, your arpeggiated palette is complete; depending on what song you're playing, it can be as dramatic or "low key" as you need.

Useful Recordings

Otis Redding Sings Soul: Otis Blue, Volt 412; *Steve Goodman, Jesse's Jig and Other Favorites*, Asylum 7E-1037.

I Can't Sleep (If I Can't Sleep With You)

3/4 Country Gospel Shuffle

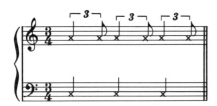

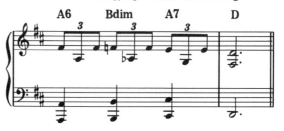

Left hand ascending, right hand descending

A6 Bdim A7 D

Linda Ronstadt was recently expounding in *Time* magazine on the difficulties of finding a drummer who could play rock *and* a good country shuffle. Actually, there are two kinds of country shuffles: the regular 12/8 rock-a-boogie kind (see p. 24) played with a lift on the last eighth note of each three-note group; and a country gospel waltz in 3/4 time. We could actually write this as 9/8, but since the straight eighth note is important, we'll leave the time signature as 3/4 and use a triplet on each quarter beat. This is a gentle, melodic style in which the drum usually accents the second and third beats of each bar with brushes or a quiet "rim shot" on the snare. A few bars of accented time look like this:

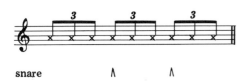

Resolutions down a fourth

Left and right hand descending

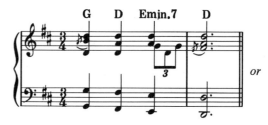

G D Emin.7 D

or

Left hand descending, right hand ascending

D C#m Bmin.7 A

"I Never Did Sing You a Love Song" by David Nichtern (writer-guitarist best known for "Midnight at The Oasis") gives us an excellent opportunity to explore a whole range of country mannerisms as they apply to the piano, the simplest and most characteristic of which is the *country resolution, up (or down) a fourth.* To make this change the country way, take the most direct route—move step-by-step, using the major scale.

Notice that you can play in either parallel or contrary motion. A good convention for when to use which would be:

1) Use the *same* motion when *beginning* a section or phrase.

2) Use *contrary* motion when *ending* a section or phrase.

Resolutions up a fourth

Left and right hand both ascending

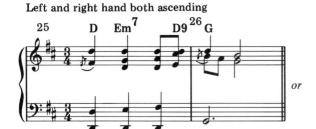

or

A7 G A7 D

Until recently, the piano was strictly a rhythm instrument in a country band (see chapter on Country Rock, p. 56)-if it was there at all. Aside from the fact that stringed instruments are traditional in country music, I'm sure the piano's position in a country band didn't reflect prejudice against it, but rather had to do with the country music milieu. Country musicians, even more than rock musicians, are constantly touring small clubs, so mobility is very important—and pianos just ain't mobile.

Increasingly now, though, since Floyd Kramer, David Briggs, and "Pig" Robbins have pioneered country lead styles, the piano has become a color as well as a rhythm instrument. Taking their cues from rock music, lead country piano styles continue to incorporate basic rhythm grooves. Here are the alternative approaches on the piano:

Playing Rhythm

When playing with a rhythm section, the left hand plays the root of the chord along with the bass guitar in a simple rendering of the meter—in this case just one-two-three, one-two-three—while the right hand articulates the finer points of the changes and rhythm with a simple figure:

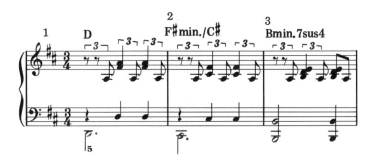

In measure 3 above, the triplet pattern is broken in the last beat by two straight eighth notes that announce a change from the groove to a moving line. Shifting the time this way is a good device that I'll use again in the next section.

Rhythm and Lead Combination

When you step out a bit more with some right-hand fills and take charge of livening up the tune, you should do so with authority but also with modesty. This can be accomplished by phrasing your melodic expansion as an *extension* of the rhythm with triplets or lines of legato eighth notes. At the same time the left hand keeps the shuffle going with a left-right rocking motion.

In general, when you're playing lead, aim for melody figures which both make the changes directly and add a little emphasis. If you have the chance, listen to Spooner Oldham's fine piano work in Maria Muldaur's recordings of this song, some aspects of which are reflected in my transcription.

It's ok to add a few blues licks in the country gospel style, so long as you play them with a stagey reverence, like quotes or inserts. There's nothing wrong with mixing idioms, but make sure to communicate clearly that your eclecticism is personal or people will become confused about the intention of your music.

Useful Recordings

Maria Muldaur, Warner Reprise MS 2148

I Never Did Sing You A Love Song

David Nichtern

Country Rock

Carl Perkins, the great country writer-guitarist-performer who wrote "Blue Suede Shoes," once told me that rock 'n' roll music was simply the result of white musicians from west Tennessee trying to play like black musicians. But this fusion of musical attitudes clearly worked both ways, and I think it's fair to say that Otis Redding and Sam Cooke wrote country songs. Compare Buddy Holly's "That'll Be the Day" with Ray Charles's "Cryin' Time," and you'll see what I'm driving at. "Cryin' Time" is a 6/8 country and western tune, and "That'll Be the Day " is a blues shuffle recently repopularized by Linda Ronstadt, who is now known as a country-pop artist. So over the years, the country input in the rock scene has been as strong and steady as the blues.

Today, country pop-rock from both L.A. and Nashville is enjoying tremendous and deserved popularity. But it has always been potentially (and sometimes actually) popular. In the golden days of rock, (1964-67) Beatle hits like "I've Just Seen a Face" and "She's a Woman" were straight country rockers. So was the Rolling Stones' "19th Nervous Breakdown." In fact, the whole Beatle vocal style was influenced more by the Everly Brothers and Elvis Presley than by anyone else.

But it wasn't until the late sixties when the West Coast rockers went country that the dam really burst. Moby Grape and the Grateful Dead were country bands. The "Dead" even had an auxilliary country rock band (The New Riders of The Purple Sage) affiliated with them. When the Byrds broke up it was in favor of The Flying Burrito Brothers and Crosby, Stills, & Nash, country-style rock bands whose vocal arrangements were bop versions of the bluegrass style. Graham Nash's "Teach Your Children Well" was at the time (1970) the first pop song in memory to feature a pedal-steel guitar. And when Bob Dylan returned from his motorcycle accident convalescence with his finest record (in my opinion), *John Wesley Harding*, it was recorded in Nashville with a Nashville rhythm section. Things haven't quite been the same since, and many of our current popular artists—The Eagles, Glen Campbell, Anne Murray, John Denver, Willie Nelson, Dolly Parton—are primarily country artists.

Within the area of country-influenced rock, certain rhythm piano grooves are used again and again, with slight variations. This chapter is written as a small country groove catalogue, with recommendations about where each groove fits.

John Denver

4
4 Country Rock Ballad
(A Los Angeles Style)

This 4/4 country rock ballad groove accounts for at least 50 percent of the country rock recorded today, especially the studio music that comes from L.A. You hear it with tempo and accent variations on songs like "Lyin' Eyes," "New Kid in Town," "Rhinestone Cowboy," "Stranger," "I'm Gonna Love You a Little Bit More," and countless others.

The two-hand interplay here is easy and fun to do. It's reminiscent of Carole King's style (page 74) except that it has a country "two-beat feel" in a 4/4 context. This is a result of having two distinct phrases per measure supported by a bass line that frequently moves to the root of the dominant (V). (See page 14)

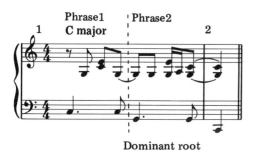

Dominant root

Constructions like this are so typical that the bass and piano in the ensemble would play exactly the same thing.

Notice the use of "hammering on" techniques used in "Rhinestone Kid" to develop phrases *internally*. This is an extremely effective way to provide color to your chording without really standing out, and is a device used extensively on the Fender Rhodes, where the ringing overtones blend into the total ensemble sound.

Lyin' Rhinestone Kid In L.A.

Country Rock Boogie

The straight-ahead rock boogie is that driving eighth note style which has come to be associated with the pure rock music of the late sixties. This playing style fits right in with the great guitar rock bands like Creedence Clearwater Revival ("Proud Mary"), or the Rolling Stones in their middle period ("Honky-Tonk Woman"), and today with the Steve Miller Band ("Keep on Rockin' Me, Baby"). I call it a country style because the simple chords are not really bluesy. Even though dominant sevenths are often used among plain voicings, they are used boldly as quotes rather than as the harmonic base.

You can see from this typical example that the rhythm constructions are aggressive and right out of early rock 'n' roll (see p. 16), tending to push the beat and the bar frequently. This is similar to the straight eighth note gospel style, but is less sophisticated and has been popularized by Nicky Hopkins. Play it vigorously and you'll be really rocking. When the crowd yells "Booogiieee!" or "Get Down!" this is what they want to hear. For right-hand improvisations, utilize the techniques developed in the chapter on Eight-To-The-Bar Rock Boogie.

Let's Spend Some Time Together

Fretted-Style Piano

Hammering on, or fretted-style piano is usually associated with Floyd Kramer but it was created decades ago by Hargus "Pig" Robbins, and has been developed more broadly by other fine country piano stylists like Bunky Keely and Charlie Rich. In the next two pieces the hammering on technique is explored in quite different ways. The example below shows it as a left-hand rhythm device. In conjunction with rolled chords in the right hand, the hammer gives a little kick to the two-beat feel and develops an internal bass line melody similar to what the rhythm guitar plays in a bluegrass band.

This groove is mostly good for sitting in with Appalachian string bands or rock bands that affect a mountain style sometimes affectionately referred to as "shit kicking music" (fertilizer is what they have in mind!) But hillbilly connotations aside, your bluegrass picking friends will be delighted that you can play in a compatible piano style.

Hammering Around

J. Gutcheon

The Talking Ballad

Red Sovine today personifies a country genre of long standing: the talking balladeer. This is someone who strums while he tells you a story. (My all-time favorite of these characters is a Canadian named Stompin' Tom Connors. Stompin' Tom comes out with his guitar and a small piece of plywood. While he shouts outrageous songs at you like "Bugs, Bugs, Bugs," or "Big Joe Muffaraw, the Meanest Man in Ottawa," he stomps the plywood to shreds. The show is over when the plywood is gone.) I've always wondered how the talking balladeer knows where he is in the song. In Red Sovine's case the answer seems to be that he has a piano player nearby who is playing a regular verse, and he follows the changes pretty much by osmosis. The example below, in 12/8 shuffle time, is similar to the piano accompaniment of Mr. Sovine's recent hit "Teddy Bear." A lovely ringing-bell quality is achieved as the hammer-on melody line moves against the chord intervals, which are tied and sustained like a pedal tone. The effect is chime-like.

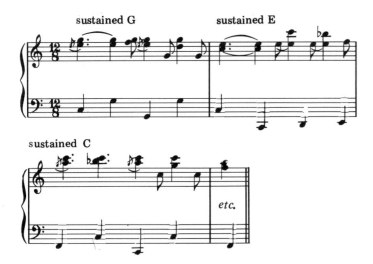

The "countriness" of this piece is assured by the total absense of accidentals, blue notes, or syncopations and off-time rhythm figures. The simplicity of this shuffle makes it one of my favorite country grooves.

Useful Recordings

Listen to your local Top 40 Country-Pop radio station. This piano style is *happening now*, and gets better every day. For country rock boogie, I still like *The Rolling Stones, Between The Buttons*, London Records, featuring Nicky Hopkins.

It Makes Me Cry

J. Gutcheon

Contemporary New Orleans Piano Styles

The Traditional Influence In New Orleans R & B

The rock 'n' roll coming out of New Orleans today continues to reflect a broad mixture of traditional and ethnic musical styles with a few new, joyful twists. The piano players currently sending the New Orleans sound abroad are Allen Toussaint (writer-producer-arranger of "Yes We Can" and "Working in a Coal Mine") and Mac Rebennack (the illustrious Dr. John of "In The Right Place.") They play with a rolling and tumbling quality which evokes a freewheeling good-time spirit and suggests some exuberant, unconventional ways the piano can be used in rock.

A Rolling Figure Used as a Hook

As we have seen, rock piano usually bolsters the central rhythm figures with closely grouped chords played percussively in the beefy lower or middle range, leaving the upper lead lines for occasional hot licks or for other instruments.

In "Let's Make a Better World" by Earl King (remember the oldie "Weary Silent Night"?) this tendency is reversed. The typical New Orleans two-beat rhythm (see p. 14) and changes are made by continuously rolling from the left hand to the right, rather than by a punctuated left-right rhythm as above.

Example A

You can notice from the comparison above that the strong beats (one and three) are now being pushed by the *outside note* (5th finger) of both hands and not by the right-hand chord. The change itself is played with the grace-note lick in the rolling motion, and the lick becomes a hook figure by adapting the same construction to all the changes. Using the entire range of the piano this way adds fullness to the ensemble sound by taking advantage of all the piano's overtones. The rhythm gets a lift from the repetitive single notes in the upper register, which cut through as well as any mid-range chord.

Left-hand Barrelhouse Technique

The left-hand technique used in this piece is a rock adaptation of the barrelhouse style popular in the Southern honky-tonks during the thirties. This was a kind of bluesy ragtime, but the unschooled players couldn't quite play a rigorous rag bass, which required alternating a single low note with a chord an octave or so above it.

Regular ragtime bass

Instead they devised a way of simulating the rag bass without ever taking their hand off the piano. This is called a walking bass.

Walking bass

This construction quite naturally led to a funkier version moved ahead by an eighth note.

or

If you now go back to Example A you can see that this bass, minus the *and*-two and *and*-four beats (left open for the snare shot) is exactly what the left hand plays in "Let's Make a Better World." In the second verse, the barrelhouse effect is heightened by rolling tenths (bars 11-20). This piece is fun to play and should get you going 'round and 'round with a Mardi Gras giddiness. And if you get a chance, I recommend that you listen to Dr. John's fine rendtion of the song on his Atlantic album *Desitively Bonnaroo*.

Useful Recordings

Dr. John, Desitively Bonnaroo, ATCO SD 7043
Dr. John, In The Right Place, ATCO SD 7018
In general; any records featuring *The Meters* as rhythm section, or recorded at Marsaint Studios in New Orleans.

Dr. John (Mac Rebennack)

Let's Make A Better World To Live In

Introduction

Earl King

repeat chorus, then repeat entire song as a "round"

The Latin-American Influence

There is a persistent Latin-American streak in New Orleans music and it shows up in every generation beginning with Jelly Roll Morton's Fandangos. "Mos' Scocious" by Mac Rebennack (Dr. John), New Orleans' emissary to contemporary rock music, is a tune which combines a Latino verse with a rock release, which gives us a chance to study some Latin constructions.

The principle ingredient in the Latin feel is *momentum,* as opposed to "drive"—that is, the groove should feel as if it is being drawn along effortlessly or even self-propelled, rather than "pushed." "Mos' Scocious" achieves this kind of motion in several ways. The main verse figure is a two-bar melody-chord sequence which is repeated once to make a four-bar rhythm sequence.

Fig. 1

Notice that the chord changes are made with the thumb in a *descending* lead line. Downward motion looks and feels easier to play because it seems to work *with,* not against, gravity.

The rhythm sequence adds to the momentum by placing the pushes of the melody line right *behind* the backbeats. In effect, this is like an extra shove to a wagon that's already rolling. The rhythm sequence is written out below in eight notes with carats marking the pushes and backbeats. Clap this rhythm out, emphasizing the carats.

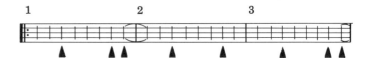

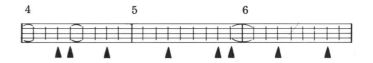

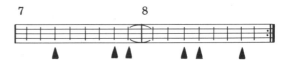

Still another kick comes from doubling up on the pushes in the second half of each four-bar figure. Since there is also a push in the first bar of the repeat, the rhythm gets quite kicky at each turnaround. Now play Figure one around several times to get into the groove.

Stevie Wonder's song "Don't You Worry 'Bout a Thing" employs a similar minor motif with a descending line, although the changes don't evolve as far. Since this is only the introductory figure in the tune, it is restricted to two bars. To build up momentum quickly, the melody pushes beat *three* halfway through the first bar, and *every beat* thereafter until the last beat of the second bar. The movement is terrific.

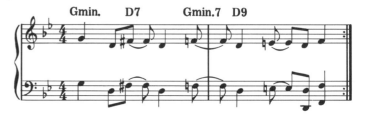

Roy Bird, alias "Professor Longhair," is the ancient New Orleans piano player who most contemporaries claim as their major influence. Much of his playing contains a Latin strain. Here is the main lick from his recording of "Big Chief." In this case, the syncopated kick is in the descending line in the left hand, while the right hand plays typical New Orleans arpeggiated swirls.

play as a "round"

In my transcription of "Mos' Scocious" I develop the syncopation of the main four-bar figure in a slightly different way each time the verse recurs to reflect these additional examples; it gets successively pushier to keep up the momentum of the groove. Most musicians I know who make recordings generally agree that a good track must gain energy and only *appear* to speed up, without actually doing so. You may want to practice these verse sections separately before trying the whole piece.

The release is straight eighth note rock 'n' roll, but the right hand demonstrates how Dr. John's bluesy finger slides can be used to move through some standard changes.

Useful Recordings

Ditto the last chapter, plus any *Professor Longhair* records for reference, and *Stevie Wonder, Innervisions,* Tamla, T326L

Professor Longhair (Roy Bird)

Mos' Scocious

Mac Rebennack

The Pop Style Of Carole King

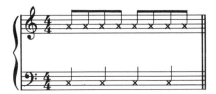

Carole King's music has been with us for quite a while. In collaboration with Jerry Goffin, she has written numerous beloved hits such as "Will You (Still) Love Me Tomorrow?" and "You Make Me Feel Like a Natural Woman." So it was a great pleasure, as well as an important musical moment, when she emerged in the early 1970s as an excellent and unique piano stylist.

Ms. King plays in a rolling eighth note style with some familiar syncopated rock mannerisms and brief, memorable melody figures known as "hooks." Her playing includes few flourishes, and she makes very direct chord changes. I think it's fair to say that Carole King's piano style has influenced recent playing, both electric and acoustic, as much as her writing has influenced a whole generation of pop songs. Clearly her knack for simple, unadorned piano arrangements is one clue to her success as a songwriter.

Carole King is always associated with the pop sound of Los Angeles, where she currently resides. However, her harmonic palette more often reflects the soul-jazz New York environment where she grew up in the 1940s and 1950s. One example is her use of major seventh chords in tandem:

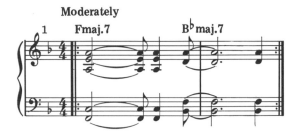

In this harmonic setting, major sevenths easily combine with minor sevenths used as passing chords:

Minor sevenths with altered roots also become the "suspensions" Ms. King frequently uses in her resolutions, instead of the usual dominant to tonic.

conventional resolution

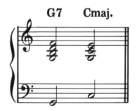

Carole King's resolution

I'm sure you recognized this sound right away. Note that the suspension may be written in two ways: G (9)sus4, where the C is the "sus4" in the G(9) chord; or Dmin7/G, which means a Dmin7 in the right hand with G played in the bass. I prefer to use the "sus4" notation.

Having fixed a few of these open, sophisticated harmonies in your mind, play this chain of Carole King chords. Since the melody or lead note simply changes back and forth from A to G, listen to the rich variety of tones that comes from the same few notes in different combinations.

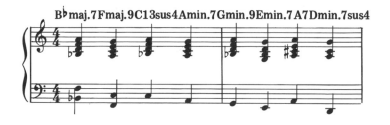

Rhythmically, Carole King is just an easy-going rock 'n' roller. Her left hand plays the quarter beats, rocking back and forth between fifth finger and thumb, while her right hand generally stresses the beat, but the thumb plays off the beat.

As you can see, she reverses rhythm for dramatic emphasis and both hands play the snycopation together. This urges the song along by pushing the next chord change ahead an eighth note, pushing the beat in typical rock fashion.

Now try this lovely Pat Alger tune, "Hurricane In Your Heart," which lends itself well to Carole King's style of playing.

Useful Recordings

Anything by Carole King, but I still like *Tapestry*, Ode, SP 77099, the best. With careful listening, you can pick her style up right from the record.

Hurricane In My Heart

Moderate

Patrick Joseph Alger

Intro

One-Note "Linear" Grooves

One-note "linear" grooves are electric piano or synthesizer lines—hooks—which are used at the head (beginning) of a tune and then continue to form the basis for the whole rhythmic groove built on top of them. They are constructed to generate a strong clear pulse, which they do both rhythmically and melodically by the use of repetitive themes. Before reading any further, glance at the examples I have chosen and you'll know immediately what I'm talking about.

Right Place, Wrong Time

Mac Rebennack

Higher Ground

Stevie Wonder

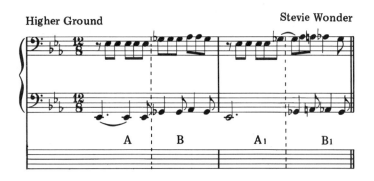

Melodic-Rhythmic Analysis

These are typically blues lines played in the upper bass; they're called "riffs" because they are repeated over and over (whereas a lick is usually used just once).

Each line is two measures long, and each of these measures is divided into two (generally—but not always) equal parts.

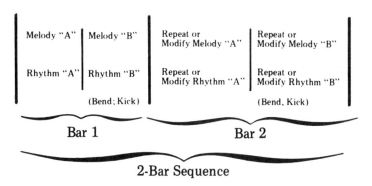

As you can see from the above diagram, these riffs are little two-part melodies, A & B. Each melody is stated in the first bar and then developed or simply repeated in the second.

The rhythmic pattern set up in the first part of each bar is altered in the second part to provide motion. This gives a little kick to the way the time feels, and is sometimes known as a "bend." *Contrast* provides the key to bending a measure well. Several good devices for altering rhythmic patterns are:

1) Change from straight time to syncopation
2) Change from syncopation to straight time
3) Double the tempo
4) Cut the tempo in half
5) Maintain the tempo but push the second section
6) Combinations of the above

Electric Pianos and Recording Techniques

As the musical principles involved in one-note linear grooves are relatively simple, this is an appropriate place to mention certain aspects of electric pianos and recording studio techniques which come into play when using those grooves. Often the ones you hear on a record can't be duplicated in a live situation by one individual (unless he has three hands).

Electric pianos fall into two categories: a) those in which the tone reeds are *struck* by hammers like regular pianos (Fender Rhodes, Wurlitzer) and b) those in which the reeds are *plucked* like a harpsichord (Hohner Clavinet, RMI Electra Piano). The ones in the second category are generally used to play linear grooves because their *pizzicato* effect is highly compatible with stringed instruments, and the plucking puts a percussive edge on the tone which cuts through other sounds very well.

Piano Action vs. Organ Action

The plucked-reed electric pianos—Hohner and RMI—are not played like a regular piano but rather like an organ because of the difference in the action. In regular piano action, the harder you hit the note, the harder the hammer hits the string (or reed) and the *louder* the note sounds. This is true of the piano-action Fenders and Wurlitzers. The Hohner and RMI have a "trip" action, so that once you depress the note a certain distance, it will automatically sound at the volume preset by your amplifier. Electric organs, which have tone generators, operate on the same principle: once the depressed note makes contact, a tone sounds until the note is released. Thus, you must play these instruments with precision and deliberation; there should be nothing at all tentative about your attack.

Rhythm and/or Feeling

As rhythm instruments, the plucked-reed electric pianos are good for funky grooving, but not for solos because you can't do much to change the color or feeling of what you play. The Fenders and Wurlitzers, on the other hand, make a softer, wider sound which can get pretty punchy and beefy at full volume. They also have beautiful, full, rich tones and a bell-like quality which is excellent for legato playing and for laying a chunky rhythm or chord pad underneath an ensemble sound. I prefer them for their attack flexibility and because they permit a wider range of emotional expression. But then, it depends on your attitude, and mine favors acoustic piano styles.

Keyboard synthesizers can produce an enormous variety of sounds but until recently could only make one sound at a time, so up to now they have been used mainly for special recording effects.

Multiple Channel Recording

Multiple channel recording techniques permit you to build up a sound by recording on top of (but not erasing) something you have already recorded. These techniques have been used to great effect in increasing the power of linear grooves on many records (I've done it myself). The best-known of these is Stevie Wonder's *"Superstition."* I may be wrong, but I'm pretty sure I hear three separate Clavinet tracks. Here are the three layers, which I've separated from each other.

The second line played over the first line.

The third line played over lines 1 & 2

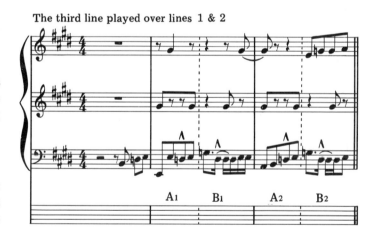

Obviously you can't get up on stage and play this all at once. But if you're recording, the above chart gives you an excellent methodology for recreating something similar. To show you what kind of a pulse this makes in terms of shear weight of the signal on tape, the following diagram gives you a graphic read-out, with the backbeat included.

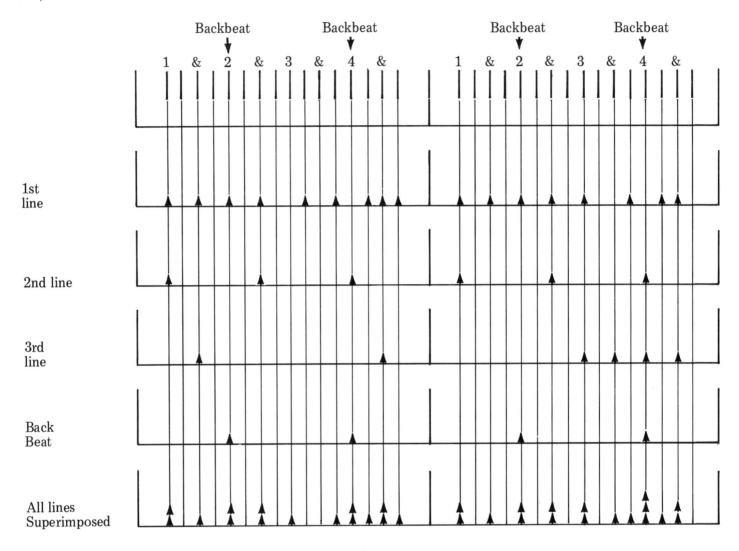

This kind of analysis helps reveal the inner musical workings of a genius like Stevie Wonder. Given a two-bar sequence to develop, he holds back slightly in the first, insistently pushes the turn into the top of bar two, keeps up the power through the third beat of the second bar, really hits the second backbeat (beat 4), and then recedes slightly to begin again. Here is what good rock is all about—*controlling* power and sustaining musical interest.

Half-Time Pop Piano Styles
Hard Rock Period

Something curious happened to rock tempos in the late sixties and early seventies, the period we now associate with hard rock and what was known in the trade as "power trios" like Cream, The Jimi Hendrix Experience, and Mountain. These "heavy" groups evolved a style of playing in which a measure of music was *nearly twice as long*, in actual time value, as ordinary boogie rhythm. In this style, the backbeat seemed to come *half* as often, and what was formerly an eighth note was now a sixteenth note. Cutting the rhythm in half this way is known as playing in half-time.

Regular bar at ordinary tempos

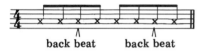

Half time bar at same tempo

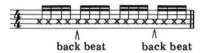

The half-time style was the rock guitar player's heaven. At last, tempos were slow enough to play *lots and lots of notes*, which guitarists loved because they played them so easily, *one at a time*, at incredibly high volume levels. Even today, the catchy Allman Brothers style of solo lines in thirds is executed by *two* guitars. The only guitarists who have seriously adopted a *chordal* solo style are Amos Garrett and George Harrison.

(Everybody said Harrison's chord melodies on "And Your Bird Can Sing" were triple-track recording. Maybe so, but I saw him do it live in Boston on the 1964 Beatles tour.)

This feedback-level, linear style of play at distended tempos really left no room for the piano: actually, the only keyboard which could compete at that volume was the Hammond B-3 organ, the centerpiece of groups like The Vanilla Fudge or Traffic. Were it not for the soul music of that era—those Stax-Volt, Motown, and Atlantic records—the piano might have disappeared from rock. Fortunately for us piano lovers, Leon Russell and Elton John successfully applied our instrument to the popular style, and the piano slowly worked its way back to the center of the rock ensemble, where it remains. The half-time fad has receded now, but its impact, especially on aspiring songwriters, has been enormous.

The half-time style is an upbeat and generally "pushy" two-handed rhythm style—pushy in the sense that a lot of beats get pushed, sometimes three or four per measure. It can be a good style for adding power to a rhythm section, but only if the tune permits a half-time feel.

To play the half-time style successfully, you have to train yourself to hear and feel the four sixteenth notes in each quarter note automatically, because the sixteenth note is the basic unit of *expressed* time in the syncopation. This is a very *busy* pulse to be counting, and it may require you to be a bit more nervous or edgy than your normal body rhythms allow.

The Half-Time Style Of Elton John

Both Elton John and Leon Russell have enjoyed tremendous success as recording artists. Elton John's half-time style, especially, is constructed with recording in mind. This means that his piano arrangements are structured to convey a *deliberate, programmed intensity* which will make songs develop at a pace that is at once logical and dramatic. It is music intended to captivate and hold your attention for about three minutes—the average per-tune airplay time allotted by top-40 radio stations—and to sound the same on either a stereo set or a car radio.

The key to improvising in this style is to divide the song up into sections and conceive a coherent, sequential development of each part. To analyze a particular song before you groove, you must:

1) Listen carefully to its lyrics
2) Try to get a feeling for
   a) where it is spare, and where full;
   b) where to hold back and where to let go, and at what rate;
   c) where other instruments might be added or play the lead.

These considerations are generally spelled out in a studio by the producer, who uses a chord chart as a road map for playing the song. If you aspire to write songs like Elton John's, this kind of discipline is essential to success. Take it from me, your auditions for record companies, booking agents, and managers will go much better if they see that your material is *organized*, and your playing *already sounds* like the piano track from the record you hope to make!

Below is a chart for this Elton John-like study piece I have constructed with the kind of notation you might actually make.

Playing the Verses

Now that you have a broad sketch of the piece, consider the dynamics of two-handed rhythm play. How you treat the backbeat determines the motion of the song. If you want to hold back the rhythm, as in the verses of this example piece, *de-emphasize* the backbeat by playing a figure which places the accent somewhere else.

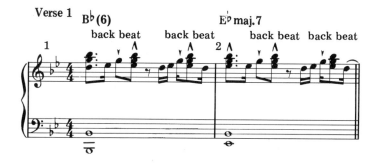

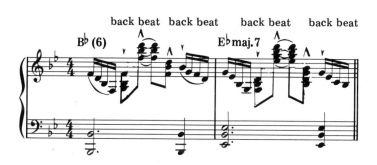

Notice these already-familiar elements of Elton John's style. His right-hand constructions simply combine arpeggios with Carole King's rocking left-side, right-side hand motion. Interest is added by changing chord inversions and melodic leads in both bass and treble.

As the chart progresses, you want to start "raving up" (English rock slang for playing more intensely), creating a sense of anticipation about the main groove that's going to hit in the chorus release. Thus in measures 7 and 8 the song is urged forward by pushing the second backbeat with a follow-up accent.

Playing the Choruses

The level of intensity reached in measure 8 is now sustained with minor variations throughout the first chorus by *playing* the first backbeat, and kicking the *second.* (Take it slowly at first because reading the two-handed syncopation can be tough. Once you understand the method, feel free to take off from the chart.)

Now you're halfway through the song and have developed the second verse with some more ornate lyrical passages (measures 20, 21). How would you go about intensifying the second chorus even more, and sustaining it? The answer is simple: *push both backbeats*—that's the final card you've been holding up your sleeve, so play it!

Studio Techniques Applicable to the Half-time Style

A discussion of half-time studio techniques now becomes relevant, because even at half-time tempos, a sixteenth note is a short space of time. When signal limiting, delayed tone decay, and a broad echo characteristic are applied to the piano track in the overall mix, what you end up hearing is *one very fat backbeat.* In reality, that one backbeat is being *pushed, played, followed up, reinforced, and sustained*—often through a whole quarter note—by virtually every instrument in the ensemble.

Thus what makes for an apparently beefy sound coming through a small speaker is in fact a large group of complex signals that have been skillfully treated in a sophisticated studio. To achieve these effects on your own piano, the best you can do is to use the sustain pedal liberally but judiciously.

Useful Recordings

Elton John is a very broadly based piano player, but his unique halftime style shows up best in his early records. Pick your favorite.

Pocket Man

J. Gutcheon

The Half-Time Style Of Leon Russell

Leon Russell is a brilliant, eclectic rock 'n' roller with a whole grab bag full of hyper-energized rhythm tricks which encompass American music from ragtime gospel to Bo Diddley. Without a doubt his guitar playing has influenced his piano style. Rhythm figures such as these are "picker's" licks:

and

In my opinion, Mr. Russell develops his programmed intensity in a way which is more organic and natural to the piano than Elton John does. Within any section of a tune, each succeeding bar grows from and modifies the rhythmic structure of the previous one, creating a kind of hierarchy of intensity which can be expressed as in the example below. Tap each rhythm out over and over in sequence until it becomes easy; then tap the next one. When you master them all, beat out the entire ladder in two-bar phrases. Empty staves are provided for you to continue the development on your own.

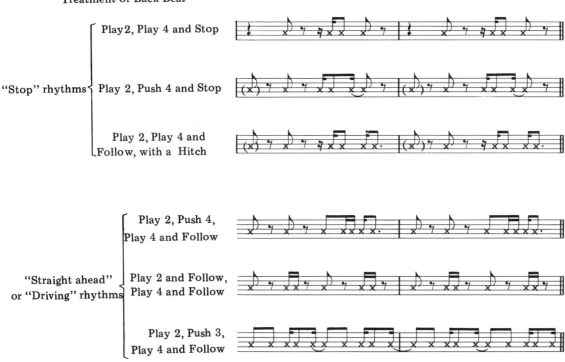

86

Now play measures 1-8 of "Shootin' Through" to put these rhythms into action. As the song develops, each new section either starts from a slightly higher place on the ladder than the last or makes a radical shift.

The great thing about this approach to rhythm piano playing is that it provides you with a ready catalogue of rhythm figures that you can deploy (as your song requires) by moving up or down in intensity. Here is an opportunity to find a piano application of any rhythm figure you hear, whether it comes from an R&B horn chart, a subway train, or galloping horses. The possibilities are endless , and depend only on your imagination and sensitivity to the rhythm of your environment. What better indication could there be that rock is a living art form?

Octave Blues Licks

As the excitement of a tune builds, Leon Russell frequently erupts with octave blues runs in his right hand while playing straight-time counterpoint with his left. There are jazzy melodies spun around the chord changes, like the solo break in bars 17 and 18. The only rule I would suggest for making such runs is: try to keep within the blues modality as described in the chapter on Blues Harmony.

Leon Russell

Shootin' Through

Brightly moderate

J. Gutcheon

solo break

to get the correct flow
repeat many times

As an afterthought, I can't resist pointing out the similarity between Leon Russell's solo breaks and ragtime. It calls to mind some of the legendary backup playing that James P. Johnson did for Bessie Smith and the Bessema Singers in *On Revival Day*, (1930, reissued by Columbia). You could just as plausibly play the solo break from "Shootin' Through" to a Ragtime bass.

This seems like a fitting place to end for the moment — tying across to that original syncopated American brothel (read "lounge") music that proper people considered lewd and that drove the young kids wild. Jelly Roll Morton, New Orleans' most notorious ragtime piano man, travelled to St. Louis, Kansas City, Memphis, Chicago, and finally settled in Los Angeles. Leon Russell hails from Tulsa, Oklahoma, has toured the world, and lives in L.A. Have they shared a common odyssey? I think so.

Taking the long view, our technology may be all that has changed. A century is scarcely a moment in the lifetime of the human spirit. So I consider it most likely, if not Mos' Scocious, that 100 years from now rock will blend right in with the rags as simply another stage in the development of an even funkier American music.

Useful Recordings

Best of Leon, Shelter SRL 52004, has most of the hits. For a taste of how crazy it really was onstage in 1970, don't miss *Mad Dogs and Englishmen*, A&M SP 6002: and for a wide sampling of Leon Russell as a fine accompanist, listen to *The Best of Freddy King*, Shelter SR 2140.

Appendix

Keeping In Shape For Rock Piano Playing

Rock piano playing can be strenuous physical exercise. If you're not in proper shape, you may begin to lose your edge at the end of an energetic set, just when you need it most. Remember that rock performances are usually at night. This means that your day is often twelve hours out of phase with everyone else's. You should be coming into your peak energy around 9:00 P.M. instead of 9:00 A.M., so arrange your nutrition and rest schedules accordingly and avoid stimulants which have a depressant aftereffect.

Consistently good rock piano playing requires both strength and flexibility in the shoulders, forearms, wrists, and hands. Hearing the beat correctly is one thing; but playing it perfectly time after time is a real challenge. Of course, playing at least an hour or two every day is essential for good "chops." In addition, here are some light exercises to keep your shoulder-arm-hand systems toned up. Use a five-pound dumbbell, which is light enough to develop your strength without making you musclebound or tight. About 20 repetitions once a day should do.

For Shoulders and upper back

For the forearms and wrists: curls, and reverse curls.

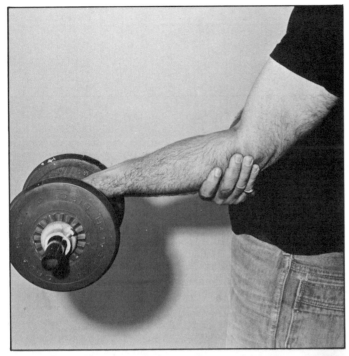 

To keep your fingers trim while you're not playing, use the rubber devices used by tennis players to improve their grip, only *don't* squeeze them tightly or hold them for long periods of time. The correct method is: lightly squeeze, hold briefly, let go; repeat for a few minutes at most (below). Doing this several times a day will keep your fingers, hands, and wrists strong but sufficiently loose. Unlike classical music or jazz, rock requires no conventional finger dexterity. In fact, most classically trained pianists find they have to "unlearn" their classical technique to play the kinds of slides and finger constructions found in rock licks.

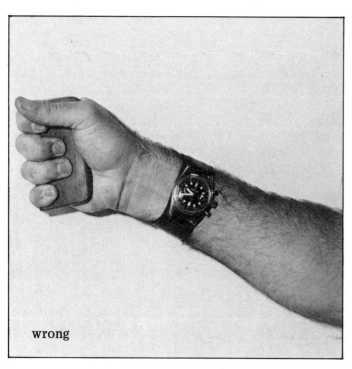

wrong

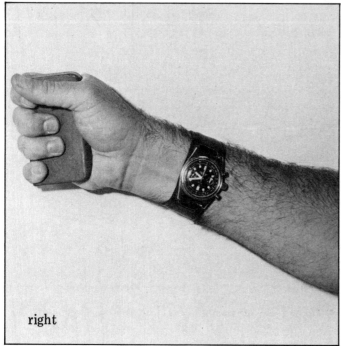

right

Improving Your Nerve Tone

Having the right musculature for rock piano playing is only one part of being able to play fast. A healthy nervous system is also essential because it delivers the "play" message to your fingers. You can help yourself achieve jangle-free nerves with nutritional aids and a particular Yoga exercise called the "plough."

A balanced daily vitamin dose is always recommended. At the very least, make sure you get 200 International Units of Vitamin E (good for the heart, too) and a good B-complex assortment, for your nerves. The best organic way to get *all* the B vitamins is by mixing two tablespoons of yeast (Brewer's or Torula) with sufficient juice to cover the nasty taste. If your diet is sugar-heavy, like many Americans', you'll find this daily regimen liberates you from the sweet craving, and yields a natural energy high.

The plough is a Hatha Yoga exercise in which you lie flat on your back, slowly raise your straightened legs to an upright position, and then proceed to bring them back over your head until your toes touch the floor (below). Then slowly return. Everyone can do this, although it may be a little tough at first.

This is the greatest neck-stretcher I know of, and here's why you need it. The nerve ganglia that send the muscle-activating impulses to your hands come out of your brain *between* the upper neck vertebrae, and proceed across your shoulders and down your arms. These same vertebrae are also carrying the weight of your head, so the space between them tends to get narrower with time, causing pressure on the nerves and muscular ineffienciency. This condition can be further aggravated by neck muscle tension. Do the plough once a day, and you'll keep a clear nerve path open between your brain and your hands.